COVENANT COMMUNITY AND CHURCH

Covenant Community and Church

A Statement on Catholic Covenant Community and a Selection of Documents

Edited by
Stephen B. Clark

Servant Publications
Ann Arbor, Michigan

Copyright © 1992 Stephen B. Clark
All rights reserved.

Published by Servant Publications
P.O. Box 8617
Ann Arbor, Michigan 48107

Cover design by Gerald Gawronski

92 93 94 95 96 10 9 8 7 6 5 4 3 2 1

Printed in the United States of America
ISBN 0-89283-806-X

Contents

Index to Abbreviations of Church Documents / 7

Part I: A Statement on Catholic Covenant Community / 9
Preface / 11
One: Covenant Community in the Catholic Church /15
   1. The Church / 15
   2. Renewal / 18
   3. Covenant Community / 20
   4. Relations to Others / 22
Two: Covenant Community and Church Authority / 25
   1. Hierarchy and People / 25
   2. The Status of Covenant Communities / 27
   3. Governmental Authorities in Community and Church / 30
Three: Covenant Community and the Liturgy / 35
   1. Holiness and Worship / 35
   2. Daily Worship and Prayer / 38
   3. Covenant Community and Sacraments / 41
   4. The Eucharistic Assembly / 42
   5. The Sacraments of Initiation / 44
   6. The Sacrament of Penance / 45
   7. Marriage / 46
   8. Conclusion / 48
Afterword / 49

Part II: A Selection of Documents / 51
Introduction / 53
   Selection One / 57
   Selection Two / 58

Selection Three / 60
Selection Four / 63
Selection Five / 71
Selection Six / 75
Selection Seven / 78

Index to Abbreviations of Church Documents

AA	The Decree on the Laity
AG	The Decree on the Missionary Activity of the Church
CD	The Decree on the Bishops
CIC	The Code of Canon Law
CL	*Christifideles*
DE M	Directory for Ecumenical Matters
DV	The Constitution on Divine Revelation
GILH	General Instructions on the Liturgy of the Hours
LG	The Constitution on the Church
SC	The Constitution on the Sacred Liturgy
UR	The Decree on Ecumenism

Part One

A Statement on Catholic Covenant Community

Preface

COVENANT COMMUNITIES ARE A NEW FORM of Christian life, one which the American Catholic Bishops called "a new development of major importance." At the same time, like most new developments in the Church, they have been controversial on occasion. This past year witnessed both the approval and commendation of a group of covenant communities by the Council for the Laity at Rome and controversies that involved the original covenant communities in North America. Both events indicated the need for a presentation of the nature of covenant community and of its relationship to the Church.

This small book contains two items intended to help the further development of covenant communities and their integration into the life of the Catholic Church. The first is a statement entitled "Covenant Community and Church." The second is a selection of documents which were influential in the establishment of covenant communities.

"Covenant Community and Church" was originally written as a draft document for the Christ the King Association, an international lay association of Catholics. This document was designed to situate covenant communities in the life of the Catholic Church. It was also designed to indicate the principles for relating them well to the Church as a whole and for having an authentically Catholic covenant community life. It was meant to accompany a statement of community order which would describe more practically how Christian communities could be built up.

In fact, "Covenant Community and Church" was not used by the Christ the King Association. We decided instead to write an expanded statement of community order that was specifically for the association. Now that that has been completed, I am publishing "Covenant Communities and Church," because it contains helpful material that is not included in the Christ the King Association statement of community order and that could help both those in Christ the King Association and outside of it.

The origin of "Covenant Community and Church" explains something of its nature. It is, first of all, a statement, not an exposition. It was intended to provide a short summary of what a covenant community in the Catholic Church should be, not to provide a developed understanding of covenant community, much less an apologetic for it.

As a statement, "Covenant Community and Church" contains many references to the current official documents of the Catholic Church. It could have drawn upon much other material, material from the rich Catholic tradition of community life, from theological writings, and from papal instructions. It was felt, however, that in such a short statement, the references should primarily be to the current official documents. That would have the added advantage of making the document useful as a guide for finding the basis of various aspects of covenant community life in these documents.

Second, "Covenant Community and Church" is a general statement. It contains no references to Christ the King Association. Its subject is simply covenant community life. Over the years, divergent approaches to covenant community life have developed. The aim of the book, therefore, has been to consider the variety of possible types of covenant communities and not to give a particular approach to covenant community, although it may not be acceptable at all points to those who use the term "covenant community" to describe themselves.

Finally, "Covenant Community and Church" is not simply

a personal document. It is a working draft for a corporate statement that incorporates suggestions from many people. It was referred to several theologians and canonists for input. Their comments were very helpful and more of them would have undoubtedly been used for the text had we worked further on the document. We were very grateful for their time and assistance.

After we decided that we needed a different sort of document, I decided to publish this one. I tried to make it clearer and more readable, but I also tried to leave it as a consensus document to which many others contributed. I, of course, bear the sole responsibility for the determination of what went into the final version of this statement and so must take the normal responsibility for its deficiencies.

I have added to "Covenant Community and Church" a selection of documents that have been influential in the development of covenant community life. There is an introduction to the selection which explains the rationale used in making it. The degree of hierarchical and theological support for what has come about may be a surprise to some.

We find ourselves entering a new era in the Catholic Church. Although that era began with the Second Vatican Council, it was also necessitated by the great changes in modern society. These changes do not look like they will come to an end in the near future, nor is it clear exactly what the new era of Catholic life will bring. "Cultural Catholicism" seems increasingly a phenomenon of the past. A pluriform church in a religiously pluralistic worldwide society seems to be in prospect.

In a way that many have not yet realized, as a response to the new situation, the Catholic Church since the Second Vatican Council has developed a broad framework of common life. This framework allows for an unprecedented variety of forms and approaches within a universal Church that is one in faith and morals.

In such a situation, covenant communities have flourished

in great variety and will probably develop even more varieties. Perhaps covenant community life will turn out to have been providentially designed as one instrument for allowing the adaptation of the ancient tradition of special ecclesial communities to undreamed-of circumstances, an adaptation capable of maintaining a faithfulness to Christian life in its wholeness.

ONE

Covenant Community in the Catholic Church

1. THE CHURCH

The eternal and all-glorious God, the Father almighty, created the whole world for his glory. He created the human race to share in his own life and to serve him, ruling over all creatures. Even when the human race disobeyed him and lost his friendship, he did not abandon his own creation, but sought to return it to his original purpose.

In Abraham God promised to bless all nations. At Sinai he chose a people for himself to witness to his faithfulness and truth. In the fullness of time, he sent his Son, Our Lord Jesus Christ, to be the savior of the world. Through his life, death and resurrection, Christ redeemed the human race, destroying death and restoring life. That we might live for the purpose for which we were created, the Holy Spirit was sent by the Father through the Son as the promised gift of blessing to complete the work of the Son on earth and to bring us the fullness of grace.

Throughout his work of re-creation, it has pleased God to make men and women holy and save them not merely as individuals without any mutual bonds, but by making them into a single people, a people which acknowledges him in truth and serves him in holiness (LG 9). The Israel of the old covenant was the original revelation of God's purpose to have a people for himself, a holy nation, a royal priesthood (Ex 19:5-6). However, even before the foundation of the world God chose us in Christ to be his sons and daughters, priests before him (Eph 1:4-5). Those he chose, he redeemed, justified, sanctified and reconciled to God as one body in Christ (Eph 1:12).

The Church of Christ is the vehicle of God's purpose, the instrument of God's plan. By its service of God in the world, especially by its missionary service of calling the human race to return to its Father and to find life in God's Son, the Church of Christ furthers God's plan. But even more, it fulfills God's purpose for the human race by what it is. In its life, in its very existence, it is the household of God, a holy temple to the Lord, a dwelling place of God in the Spirit (Eph 2:19-22). As such, the Church is the initial budding forth on earth of the kingdom of God (LG 5), a sign of that union with God which is his plan for the human race (LG 1), a plan that will only be fully accomplished when Christ comes again and God is everything to everyone (1 Co 15:28).

Those human beings who respond to God's call through the gospel of Christ receive their share in the fulfillment of God's purpose by being built into the holy temple so that they might be a dwelling place of God in the Spirit (Eph 2:22). Their Christian life, then, is a partnership with other Christians in which they share the same inheritance, claim the same promise and belong to the same body; for Christ has only one (Eph 3:6). In entering into communion with one another, they enter into communion with God (1 Jn 1:3).

What the Church is in Christ can only be fully seen by the eyes of faith, because it is established in heavenly places and exists through the Holy Spirit (Eph 1:3, 2:18). At the same time, the Church is visible now because the Lord intends it to be the earthly expression of human life renewed in the image and likeness of the creator (Col 3:10). Even more he intends the life of the Christian people, especially in its oneness, to be something that the world, the unspiritual, unconverted world, might see and so believe in Christ's word (Jn 17:21).

To be sure, by God's design the life of the Christian Church on earth is incomplete in its realization in this age. Likewise, it is marred by the weakness and sinfulness of its human members, including its leaders, and is therefore not an unflawed accomplishment of God's purpose. God has, however, achieved in his work that which he aimed at, and his Church truly exists. The visible assembly of the Christian people and the spiritual community, the earthly Church and the Church enriched with heavenly things, are not two separate realities, but one interlocked reality comprised of a divine and human element, in a way similar to the divine and human united in Christ (LG 8). Both together are the one Church of Christ.

As an earthly, visible body of people, the Christian Church has to be ordered, with a common pattern of life and a government. If it were not, it would lack the completeness of a human community and so fall short of God's purpose for its earthly existence. In our day, however, there are many bodies of Christians ordered into churches and into ecclesial communities that live separately from one another, even though present in the same geographical locality. That might lead us to believe that the Church of Christ has lost elements essential to its oneness. However, we believe that the Catholic Church has preserved all the elements God intended it to have, and we recognize that the Catholic Church has a special place among the various Christian bodies because of the way the Church of Christ subsists in it (LG 8).

We do not deny the presence of Christ and of his truth and his sanctification in other bodies of the Christian people, but we recognize in the Catholic Church a continuation of the Church of Christ from the days of the apostles. This continuity is especially due to the preservation of the apostolic succession and the universal presidency of the first bishop, the successor of Peter at Rome. We likewise recognize that all divinely revealed truth and the fullness of salvation have been given to the Catholic Church (UR 3). We can acknowledge that greater holiness and greater Christian zeal as well as a greater appreciation for certain elements in divine revelation can be found in some of our fellow Christians who are not Catholics than we ourselves possess as individual Catholics. Nonetheless, we believe that being a member of the Catholic Church is the way to be most fully incorporated into the Church of Christ.

We therefore wish all that we do, in whatever circumstances of life, to be the expression of our life as Catholics. Some of what we do, we do as members of a secular society. Some of what we do, we do as fellow Christians with those who are not members of the Catholic Church in groupings that are not under the direct authority of the Catholic hierarchy. Some of what we do, we do as Catholics in voluntary associations with other Catholics, public or private, officially recognized or not officially recognized. Some of what we do, we do in the context of the normal structures of the Catholic Church under the presidency of the Catholic hierarchy.

Nonetheless, our life as Catholics embraces all of these situations, and we wish the way we handle these situations to be an expression of our life as Catholics. We therefore wish them to be carried out in good relationship with the governing authorities of the Catholic Church, under their authority in the appropriate way. We wish our lives and actions in these various situations to be means of extending the reign of Christ and a way for the leaven of the Catholic Church in the world to be a benefit to others.

2. RENEWAL

The Church, the body of Christ, has Christ and his Spirit dwelling within. It has every spiritual blessing in the heavenly places. Yet it is in need of renewal. It is at the same time holy and always in need of being purified. It is continually pursuing the path of penance and renewal (LG 9). Recognizing the predestined call and nature of the glorious Church of God (Eph 5:27) should not lead to a failure to recognize the actual state of the people of God and their need.

To confess that the essentials of Christian teaching and the means of salvation can be found in the Catholic Church is not to say that the actual life of the Church always adequately expresses what the Church contains. Nor is it to say that its teaching and means of sanctification always effectively reach those who are members of the Church. The gift of God leads to a call to his people to realize ever more fully in the circumstances of this life everything he has called his people to.

The renewing work of the Holy Spirit is an ongoing part of the life of the pilgrim people of God. In every age, the Holy Spirit begins movements of renewal. Sometimes he does so through the ordinary forms of church life, sometimes through special interventions that may lead to new forms of Christian living.

We live in a special time of renewal in the Catholic Church. We live after a Council that was called to accomplish a needed spiritual renewal, a renewal of its leaders and of the flocks entrusted to them. This renewal was called for so that God's glory might be revealed in the face of Christ and in his Church in a way more manifest to all men and women (Vatican Council: Opening Message).

We are called to a renewal of Catholic life through a return to the sources of scripture and tradition. We are likewise called to a Catholic life more up-to-date in the way it takes into account the current realities of our rapidly changing world. We live in an age which makes specially urgent the Church's task of bringing all men and women to full union with Christ, the light of the nations (LG 1).

We therefore live in a time in which we cannot simply rely on the accomplishments or forms of life of the past. Rather we must live the unchanging life of Christ and his Church in new ways. These have to be both more effective for our age and more faithful to what was entrusted to the Church in the beginning.

3. COVENANT COMMUNITY

As throughout the ages the Holy Spirit has been active among the Christian people to bring about renewal, groups of Christians have come together to respond. Many Christians have come together to perform some special services or foster spiritual growth with no further bond among themselves than that necessary for achieving particular goals.

But the human race is naturally social, and it has pleased God to unite those who believe in Christ in the people of God (cf. 1 Pet 2:5-10), and into one body (cf. 1 Co 12:12, AA 18). Therefore, the very nature of the Christian people is to be brothers and sisters in the Lord, one in the Spirit in the bonds of peace and mutual love (Eph 4:3). Consequently, when the Holy Spirit renews his people, he often leads groups of Christians to join themselves to one another to live more fully the life together of the Christian people. Such a coming together is not intended as an alternative to the life of the Church. Rather, it is a renewed living out of what the life of the Church should be and so signifies the communion and unity of the Church of Christ (AA 18).

In our day, desire for such coming together is felt with greater strength because of the loss of natural community in society and in Catholic parishes. With this has come the weakening of mutual help for the needs of human life and of mutual support for Christian living. The Catholic Church has recognized the existence of such a spiritual impetus among the Christian people and has sought to encourage it. Consequently, the formation of new Christian groupings is now canonically recognized by the Church. It is protected by the right to freely establish and direct special associations to foster the Christian vocation in the world (CIC, c 215).

In recent years the Lord has brought into existence new forms of Christian life that are called covenant communities. They are covenantal because they are based on the voluntary commitment of members to one another in a serious way that is not necessarily lifelong and does not necessarily partake of the nature of a vow. The commitment is in the form of a personal covenant of brothers and sisters one to another that supplements and strengthens the relationship that comes from being baptized members of the Church. They are communities because they share together their spiritual and material goods as a way of expressing their relationship as brothers and sisters in the Lord.

The relationship together of the members of covenant communities is personal and family-like, with a concern that extends to the whole of their lives. In that it contrasts to the partial and functional relationships that predominate in our society and tend to increasingly prevail in Catholic parishes and organizations. At the same time, the members' relationship to one another is not normally the kind of commitment that is found in religious communities and secular institutes, a commitment which puts the whole of each person's life under obedience to the leadership of the community. In this sense, the commitment together is a limited commitment. Those in authority in the community have the role of helping the members to live an active Christian life and to fulfill the commitments to one another they make in the covenant.

There are many types of covenant communities. Some are together primarily for mutual support in Christian life and service, while others are missionary bodies, established to be available to the work of the Lord for particular services. Some are together for the renewal of the parochial or diocesan life of the Catholic Church, while others engage primarily in an evangelistic or social apostolate in the wider society. Some are together to live a special spirituality, while others have no other spirituality than the common one of the Church. All these communities are at one in their desire to live together as brothers and sisters their Christian way of life.

To the degree that covenant communities arise out of a desire to live more fully the life of the Church, they are patterned upon that life. They look to scripture for instruction in how Christians live together and how Christian leadership functions. They likewise look to the tradition of the Church for models of how to live Christian life together and how to relate to the broader Church. They desire to live the life of the people of God in communion with the hierarchy of the Church within the limits of what Catholic teaching, Catholic canon law and special hierarchical approval allows to them.

4. RELATIONS TO OTHERS

While there are covenant communities whose members have a special life together in one location with common ownership of goods, most covenant communities are made up of Christians who live among non-Christians in the ordinary circumstances of family and social life. They engage in secular professions and occupations (LG 31). They are commonly involved with others in a variety of relationships outside the context of the covenant community.

Insofar as members of covenant communities live in secular nations, they should be subject to the government of the nation they belong to and should abide by its laws (Ro 13:5, Tit 3:1). They should be ready for any honest work, including work to improve the temporal order (AA 7, 5, Tit 3:1). They should seek to do good to all, including those not of the household of the faith (Gal 6:10). They should be especially zealous to shoulder the splendid burden of working to make the divine message of salvation known and accepted by all men and women throughout the world (AA 3).

Members of covenant communities, as members of the Christian people and of human society, should see no necessary conflict in belonging to both at the same time. Rather they should strive to harmonize the rights and duties that belong to their membership in the Church and in human society, including their responsibilities to the two authorities

(LG 36). At times they may engage as members of their covenant communities in special services to society joined with others who are not Christians. In such cases, it is preferable to do so in a way that allows joint supervision to be exercised by responsible Christians along with others.

Members of covenant communities should also recognize the great importance of unity among all Christians, one of the chief concerns of the Second Vatican Council. They should desire to cooperate in that movement which was fostered by the grace of the Holy Spirit for the restoration of unity among Christians. They do so by prayer, brotherly love, and concern for renewal in the Catholic Church, as all members of the Catholic Church should (UR 4). They also can do so by living their Catholic life in a way which, while preserving the essentials, expresses in the most effective way possible a Catholicism which is now accessible to other Christians. It therefore should appear in as Christ-centered, scriptural, and patristic a light as possible (UR 11, DV 21).

Sometimes members of covenant communities join with their brothers and sisters in the Lord who are not Catholics for joint works of Christian outreach and service. They especially join in that evangelistic and missionary outreach that can be fostered by unity among the followers of Christ. It is preferable to engage in such works with joint supervision by Catholic leaders and others. Such works should follow the ecumenical guidelines of the Catholic Church and the local dioceses.

Members of covenant communities also at times enter into brotherly relationships within a broader ecumenical community, relationships involving a bond of charity, prayer and witness with Christians or groups of Christians belonging to other confessions. When they do so, they normally form, with the approval of the bishops, Catholic associations or fellowships. The leaders of such associations share with other leaders in the supervision of the ecumenical body.

Members of covenant communities sometimes make those

in mixed marriages a special concern. They help the partners to see how there can be a life together that reaches to all things and a respect for the authority of the husband as head of the family without weakening the Christian faith of the family, compromising the faith of the Catholic partner, or failing to respect the authority of the leaders of the churches the partners belong to. Sometimes they reach out to Catholics involved in Christian outreaches led by non-Catholics, teaching them the value of their Catholic faith and supporting them in living it. In all this they seek to confess before the whole world with all Christians their faith in God, one and three, and in the incarnate Son of God, our Redeemer and Lord (UR 12).

Finally, members of covenant communities as members of the wider Catholic Church seek to be a benefit to the whole Church. Some work in and contribute to dioceses, parishes and church organizations that are not sponsored or led by the covenant community. Some promote renewal or stand for integral Christian truth in the crisis of faith in our day. All pray for the Church and live the life of members of the one Church whether within the context of the covenant community or within other contexts.

The covenant communities themselves sometimes serve corporately within the Church, although more commonly their contributions come through their members engaging directly in Church life and organizations. Even where the community as a whole does not serve corporately within the Church, they should always seek to strengthen the Church by the testimony of a renewed Christian life. The communitarian spirit of covenant communities should lead them to seek to contribute to the unity and common good of the broader people of which they are a part.

TWO

Covenant Community and Church Authority

1. HIERARCHY AND PEOPLE

For the building up of the Christian people, the Lord established ministries in his Church. Among his ministers are some endowed with sacred authority, who are servants of their brethren. They labor so that all who are of the people of God, and therefore enjoy a true Christian dignity, can work towards a common goal freely and in an orderly way, and arrive at salvation (LG 18).

Jesus, even before his death, appointed twelve apostles, presided over by Peter. These in turn before their death appointed successors to continue those aspects of their role which were not simply foundational but which were ongoing elements of the life of the Church. This included presiding in love over a people that was to be hierarchically structured (LG 18). To the place of the apostles succeeded the bishops to be teachers of doctrine, priests of sacred worship and officers of good order. The successors of those bishops, presided over by the Pope, the Bishop of Rome, govern the Catholic Church today (LG 20).

As teachers, bishops speak in the name of Christ and pass on Christian faith and morals (LG 25). As priests of sacred worship, they regulate and direct the celebration of the sacraments and represent and symbolize the charity and unity of the body of Christ (LG 26). As officers of good order, bishops have the authority to make laws for their subjects, to pass judgment on them and to moderate everything pertaining to the ordering of worship and the apostolate (LG 27).

The bishops are not the only members of the Church who teach, sanctify and govern. All full members of the Church, lay, religious or clerical, can take part in the work of teaching, sanctifying and governing with a spiritual authority proper to their position. Moreover, not everything bishops do, even when acting as bishops, is done with the full authority of their episcopal ministry. The submission that is appropriate towards bishops varies according to the nature of their actions. Nonetheless the bishops, in union with the Pope, have an essential role in presiding over the ordering of the life of the people of God. As a result, whatever is not in right relationship with the local bishop and/or the Pope is not in right relationship with the Church of Christ.

The members of the Church, the people of God under the governance of the hierarchy, are clergy, religious or laity. In principle there could be covenant communities made up of only clergy or only religious. In practice, covenant communities are made up either of all laity or of laity together with clergy and religious, with the laity numerically predominant. Covenant communities, therefore, tend to have a lay character and are commonly understood to be lay associations, even when their statutes make provision for clerical or religious members.

Insofar as the covenant community is a lay association, its life arises from the spiritual mission of the laity. As the name "laity" indicates, they are full members of the people of God (LG 31). They come together in associations to live a more perfect life, a more authentically and consistently Christian life (CIC, Can 298). They often also come together to engage in those apostolic endeavors which allow them as Christians living in the larger society, often among non-Christians or nominal Christians, to spread the kingdom of Christ over all the earth (AA 2, CIC, Can 298).

At times, members of covenant communities and, at times, whole covenant communities aid in the apostolate of the hierarchy (AA 20). However, except for such forms of apostolate, the laity do not build up their own lives spiritually and engage in apostolic activities through the delegation of the hierarchy. Rather they do so in virtue of their own vocation and position as members of Christ's faithful (LG 32, 33, CIC, Can 225).

2. THE STATUS OF COVENANT COMMUNITIES

Covenant communities may have a variety of relationships to the Catholic hierarchy (AA 24). The canonical foundation of their existence depends on the right of association within the Church (AA 19, 24, CIC, Can 214-216). The actual form of the relationships which is most fitting depends on their call as a community and the role they play within the corporate life of the Church. Correspondingly, although all Catholic covenant communities are subject to the normal government of the hierarchy, the kind of regulation and direction that they receive varies.

Some covenant communities are established by the hierarchy and are approved as a public association in the life of the Catholic Church. As such, they receive more regulation and direction from the hierarchy in accordance with the canons for public associations (CIC, Can 301, 304-309) and with their own statutes. Some covenant communities desire an official approval and a mutually agreed-upon relationship with the hierarchy and may be a private association. As such, they receive more limited supervision and care from the hierarchy in accordance with the canons for private associations (CIC, Can 299-300, 304-310, 321-326) and with their own statutes. Some covenant communities do not desire approval, but these too should be in good communication and relationship with the proper member of the hierarchy and acknowledge his responsibility for the common good and preservation of doctrine and good order within the Church. They also should recognize his duty to pass judgment as needed on any activity of theirs as to its accordance with Catholic teaching on faith and morals and with Church law (LG 27, AA 24). No community may claim the name "Catholic" without the consent of the lawful Church authority (CIC, Can 300).

Covenant communities may simply be local communities, or they may join in regional or international associations. Those that join in regional or international associations relate to the proper organ of the hierarchy for their life as an association in the broader Church. They also relate to the local ordinary or his delegate for their relationship to the local Church.

Covenant communities may also be related to the local Church in a variety of ways in regard to the meeting of the needs of their members. Some covenant communities will be allowed by their statutes or by the approval of the local bishop to be the place where the normal instructional, liturgical and sacramental functions of the Church can be obtained by their members. Some covenant communities will, with the approval of the local bishop, be a place in which some supplementary sacramental and instructional functions are provided for their members as a way of strengthening them further and integrating their life in the community with their life in the broader Church. In these cases what the community provides should not replace the normal life of the parish for its members. Some covenant communities will not be in a position to provide sacramental services for their members. In their community life and instruction they should support their members' participation in parish life and teach them how to integrate it properly with the support they find in the life of the community.

Covenant communities may likewise be in a variety of relations to the hierarchy in regard to their outreach. Some covenant communities wish to help the Church with official pastoral duties such as the teaching of Christian doctrine, certain liturgical actions and the care of souls. Such services should be fully subject to ecclesiastical direction (AA 24). Some covenant communities may be asked to work under the hierarchy in services which have an immediately spiritual purpose and receive a special mandate to do so. The authorities who authorize such services assume a special responsibility for them, although without depriving the communities of the possibility of acting on their own accord (AA 24).

Some covenant communities establish various outreaches, but do so on their own initiative and under the guidance of the wisdom they have. Such services are subject to the judgment of the hierarchy in regard to whether their activities conform to moral principles and whether supernatural values are properly protected and promoted, but they are not under the direction of the hierarchy (AA 24). Christ's faithful are free to perform such services especially when they judge that they can best serve the cause of Christ or the mission of the Church by working in such a manner. Such services may not claim the name "Catholic" without the consent of lawful Church authority (AA 24).

Many covenant communities will undertake no services as a body, but their members will engage in a variety of services, apostolic or otherwise. Moreover, most covenant communities, even when they sponsor corporate services, will have members who serve in other ways. In such cases, it is the responsibility of the members to conduct their service in the light of Catholic teaching and discipline where it may be applicable.

In order to find the proper place of the covenant community in the life of the Catholic Church, the cooperation of the leaders and of the appropriate member of the hierarchy is needed. On the one hand, since there is a right of association within the Church, the choice of the type of relationship of the covenant community to the Church belongs to the community itself seeking the form of life that is most appropriate to the call God has given it. On the other hand, since the regulation of the life of the Church belongs to the hierarchy, the approval of the type of relationship of the covenant community to the Church belongs to the proper member of the hierarchy discerning what is for the good of the Christian people as a whole, including the community itself.

3. GOVERNMENTAL AUTHORITIES IN COMMUNITY AND CHURCH

Any body of Christians needs governors to build up the body and to promote the common good so that the body can live together in an orderly way (LG 18). Just as the Church as a whole needs ministers to preside over it in love, so does a covenant community.

The ministry of the governor of a covenant community is both like and unlike the ministry of the leaders in the Church. It is unlike in that the ministry of the hierarchy and the clergy is instituted and authorized by Christ and has a sacramental nature. It is like in that the functions are similar, since the leaders of a covenant community need to teach some Christian truth to their members, need to work for their sanctification, at least by their prayer, encouragement and example, and need to govern them as a body and in a common way of life. It is, finally, unlike in that covenant communities often have some degree of sharing of life and goods and often have some degree of commonly organized Christian service for all the members. As a result the leaders of covenant communities not only share more closely in the daily life of the members but also may have to more directly oversee daily organizational matters.

To the degree that the leaders of covenant communities build up the members as Christians, their service can be described as pastoral. Sometimes the local bishop or the Pope may allow covenant communities to provide the functions of a local parish and so may integrate it into the normal structures of the Church, albeit with a special status. At other times, even when there is a priest present in the governing leadership of the community, the members of covenant communities live as part of two bodies with two sets of governors in a way traditional in the Catholic Church, not only for members of religious communities but also for members of Christian families and of nations that have considered themselves Christian nations.

The existence of the community and the relationship between the community and the ordinary structures of the Church is meant to provide greater strength for the whole Church. It can, however, only do so by eagerness to maintain the unity of the Spirit in the bonds of peace (Eph 4:3). Although the primary source of unity in the Church is the work of the Holy Spirit, there are certain conditions that need to be met by the leaders of covenant communities to maintain the bond of peace.

A first condition for unity is submission to God's truth as interpreted by the Catholic magisterium. When two governing authorities are both working to build people up in the same truth, their efforts reinforce and support one another.

A second condition for unity is the respect for the law of the Church and the duties and limitations it imposes. This means, among other things, that the governors of covenant communities cannot perform functions that they are not authorized to do by Church law and that they need to cooperate properly with those who are authorized to perform those functions. It also, however, means that the governing authorities of the Catholic Church respect the right of association and of self-government provided for in Church law.

A third condition for unity is the role of the bishop as a source of unity as representative of Christ, whether the local bishop or the Pope. It belongs to the episcopal office to so gather and mold the whole family of the flock that everyone, conscious of his own duties, may live and work in the communion of love (CD 16). It likewise belongs to the episcopal office to pass judgment as needed (LG 27). The granting of statutes or some other agreement as to the functioning of the covenant community within the larger Church is a very helpful means to unity, although even with statutes good communication is an ongoing need.

It is a great advantage for a covenant community to have the services of priests. Sometimes, these priests may exercise pastoral care of the members of the community according to the appointment of the bishop or according to the statutes of the community as an association of the faithful. Sometimes these priests may fulfill the function of a spiritual counselor to the community. Sometimes these priests will simply be members and can exercise a pastoral ministry as they are invited to do so. The governors of a covenant community may freely choose priests to serve the community from among the priests who lawfully exercise a ministry in the diocese, but priests require the confirmation of the ordinary (CIC, Can 324).

Priests may be governors within the covenant community. Their service in the covenant community as governors, however, is distinct from that of their ministry as priests. Any exercise of their ministry as priests, especially where jurisdiction is involved, is directly subject to the authority of the local ordinary and carried out in accordance with the law of the Catholic Church. On the other hand, any exercise of their service as governors in the covenant community is subject to whatever supervisory authority they may be under in the community and subject to the statutes and/or legislation of the covenant community.

Governors of covenant communities have a responsibility for the life together of the communities and for helping their members live a Christian way of life. They, therefore, have an obligation to exercise some discipline in the external forum over the lives of the members, according to the commitment of the members and the covenant and agreement of the community. They do not, however, exercise the canonical or sacramental powers of the Church by virtue of their position in the covenant community.

Governors of covenant communities should take care to exercise their disciplinary role in harmony with the teaching of the Church and to avoid impeding the lawful functioning of the sacramental and disciplinary action of the Church. They should be eager to promote fervent Christian living and solid Christian belief among the members of the community, should follow an approach to community discipline which is in harmony with Christian tradition and should respect the limits of their own knowledge and formation in the help they give.

The Church of Christ was instituted by Christ. It is governed by those who have succeeded in an orderly manner to the positions of government established by Christ. Their authority is rooted in the sacrament of orders (CL 23). The covenant community is established by the covenant commitment of its members in response to God. It is governed by those who have been chosen according to the constitution of the community. Their authority comes from the charism that gave rise to the community and from the agreement of the members of the community as expressed in the covenant (CL 24). Insofar as it is a Christian and ecclesial authority, it is rooted in the sacrament of baptism (CL 23).

The properly chosen governors of the covenant community, when they speak Christian truth and conduct themselves in a Christian manner, especially when they act with the inspiration or anointing of the Holy Spirit, exercise a spiritual authority. Their relationship to the broader Church should be expressed in the respect they show for the preeminent spiritual authority of the Catholic Church and for the positions of its governors who are to be respected and highly esteemed in love because of their work (1 Th 5:12).

THREE

Covenant Community and the Liturgy

1. HOLINESS AND WORSHIP

All those who belong to the Church, as disciples of Christ are called to holiness of life (LG 40). Justified in the Lord Jesus, baptized into him, they are sons and daughters of God and sharers in God's nature and so made holy (Gal 3:27, LG 40). As they follow in Christ's footsteps, and mold themselves in his image, seeking the will of the Father in all things and devoting themselves with all their being to the glory of God and the service of neighbor, the change in them becomes manifest in a holiness of life (LG 40).

Those who belong to the Church live the life of the age to come. Even now they partake in the same love of God and neighbor which makes up the heavenly life and sing the same hymn of glory to our God which is sung before his throne (1 Co 13:8, Rev 14:3, LG 49). Nonetheless, this life will achieve its full perfection only at the restoration of all things (Ac 3:21). Therefore they live as pilgrims longing for the coming again of Christ and the full manifestation of God's plan (LG 48, 2 Pet 3:11-12).

As the Lord in our time seeks to renew his people, he renews in them the holiness of life which he has called them to. That holiness of life is expressed in a deeper commitment to the brotherly love which forms the life together of the members of the body of Christ, but it is even more expressed in a love of God above all else. As a result, in the life of the Christian people the human is directed and subordinated to the divine, the visible likewise to the invisible, action to contemplation, and this present world to that city yet to come, which we seek (Heb 13:14, SC 2). A life of holiness therefore involves a daily life of worship and prayer, giving the Lord the honor which is his due, blessing him for his goodness, and drawing strength from his presence and grace.

The Lord called his people of the old covenant to first rebuild the temple, the place of worship, so that he might take pleasure in it, appear in his glory, and restore their fortunes (Hag 1:8). In a similar way, the renewal of Catholic life in our day began with a restoration and promotion of the liturgy, the public worship of the Church (SC 1, 14). That restoration of the liturgy, however, proves lifeless without faith and conversion. These in turn come from the preaching of the gospel and the outpouring of the Holy Spirit (SC 9). Christian renewal, then, begins with a renewal in relationship with God manifested by a life of worship and prayer that comes out of a true conversion to Christ.

As the Lord brings covenant communities into existence, they too participate in and draw vitality from a liturgical life of prayer and worship. Full liturgical and sacramental worship, however, as an expression of the Church, can only exist by hierarchical approval. For some covenant communities, the community itself can be the normal place of liturgical worship and sacramental strengthening because of its statutes or by special approval. For some covenant communities, the community will be able to provide liturgical worship and sacramental services as a supplement to normal parochial life. For some covenant communities, however, the community will not be able to provide liturgical worship or sacramental services, but its members will rely upon normal parochial life.

In all cases the community recognizes that the liturgy is

the summit towards which the activity of the Church is directed and the fountain from which it flows (SC 10). Even where liturgical functions in the proper sense (CIC, Can 834) are not a regular part of the life of the covenant community, the prayer life of the community should be derived from the liturgy, molded by it and harmonized with it (SC 13). Its prayer life should, in short, be carried on in the spirit of the liturgy.

In the spirit of the liturgy, Christian worship and prayer should be centered in a glorification of the Lord of all through his Son our Lord Jesus Christ in the Holy Spirit. It should be based on a solid appreciation of the great truths of creation and redemption, regularly brought to remembrance but especially recalled and celebrated in the seasons of the Church Year (SC 102). It should come from the scriptures or be scriptural in its inspiration, and it should foster a warm and living love for the scriptures (SC 24, 35, 121; DV 21). It should be communal or corporate in spirit, so that even when Christians pray alone or in small groups, they pray as members of the whole body of Christ, manifesting the Church (GILH 9, 22).

Christian worship and prayer as renewed by a liturgical spirit should be rooted in a desire to grow in Christian living, one that seeks effective ways to live a holy life in the changed circumstances of our times (SC 1). It should, in addition, be free from whatever could lead separated brethren into error regarding the true doctrines of the Church (LG 67). It should therefore be marked by a balanced expression of Christian truth, be well-ordered in relationship to the foundation of the Christian faith (UR 11), and be nourished from the treasures of the many traditions, past and present, which are alive in other Churches and ecclesial communities (DEM, II, 1). Finally, Christian prayer and worship as renewed by a liturgical spirit should lead to a greater desire to bring all to Christ and so increase the fervor of the Christian people for their mission (SC 1).

In the spirit of the liturgy our worship and prayer should

be shaped by the due honor which we give to those with whom we are united in Christ. Above all that honor is due to the one true God, for from him and through him and to him are all things (Ro 11:36). We honor him with supreme worship as the Father, the creator of heaven and earth. We honor the Son he sent into the world, our Lord and savior, Jesus Christ, who died and rose for us that he might bring us to his Father (1 Pet 4:18, Jn 14:6, 20:17). We likewise honor the one Holy Spirit, by whom we are given life, sanctified and made into a holy temple in the Lord (Ro 15, Eph 3:21).

At the same time, we are saved and brought to God not just as individuals, but as a people, members of that Church which embraces the living and dead. Therefore we honor those who are one with us in Christ and who have been a help to us by being the servants through whom the Church was built, especially the apostles, but others as well who carried on their work. We also honor those who left us an example of their lives and virtues, especially the martyrs. We honor with special reverence Mary, the Mother of God, who is joined by an inseparable bond to the saving work of her Son. In her the Church holds up and admires the most excellent fruit of the redemption, joyfully contemplating as in a faultless model that which she herself wholly desires and hopes to be (LG 66, SC 103).

Thanking the Lord for all these men and women of God we invoke their intercession. Together with them, as one family, in the one Church, we celebrate the praise of the divine majesty. We look forward to that day when we will all stand together before his throne and he will be all in all (Rev 7:15, 1 Co 15:28).

2. DAILY WORSHIP AND PRAYER

All those who are joined to Christ and come to the Father in him are built into a spiritual house, a holy priesthood, offering spiritual sacrifices acceptable to God through Jesus

Christ (1 Pet 2:5). Therefore, persevering in prayer and praising God they should present themselves as a living sacrifice, holy and pleasing to God (Ac 2:42-47, Ro 12:1, LG 10). Following the Lamb, they learn the new song, sung before the throne of God in worship. They join in the eternal hymn of praise to the glory of their creator and in intercession for the salvation of the whole world (Rev 14:3, SC 83). The life of a disciple of Christ should be a priestly life, a life of daily worship and prayer, a life consecrated to God by the regular offering of spiritual sacrifices of praise and prayer which acknowledge his lordship (SC 84).

The life of daily worship and praise is a continuation of the priestly work of Christ (SC 83). While the Eucharistic celebration is the main way in which the priestly service of worshiping God is continued among the Christian people, the liturgy of the hours (the divine office) is the especially recommended way to sanctify each period of time in the daily life of the Christian. So important is the liturgy of the hours that some, mainly priests and religious, are given the responsibility and the obligation to pray the hours on behalf of the whole Church (SC 84). Moreover, it is the one form of prayer canonically recommended for all the faithful (CIC, Can 1174).

Some of the laity will be able to pray the full liturgy of the hours in an official celebration at least from time to time (SC 84, GILH 27). Some will be unable to do so, but can pray certain parts of it. They can also use the liturgy of the hours to provide the model for daily prayer (GILH 27).

Worship and prayer modeled on and drawn from the liturgy of the hours follows a pattern for the consecration of time (GILH 10). Morning prayer (lauds) and evening prayer (vespers) are the two main forms of prayer consecrating each day, following the pattern of the daily worship of the temple (Ex 29:38-39). They can be supplemented by one or more shorter times of prayer during the day and one at the end of the day. In addition, a time of spiritual reading and meditation can be a regular means of growth in spiritual wisdom and understanding.

The week is consecrated by the celebration of the Lord's day, the day of the resurrection, on Sunday, especially through the Eucharistic assembly, but also with appropriate psalms, prayers and readings (SC 106). The week is additionally consecrated by a commemoration of Friday as the day of the crucifixion. Finally, the year as a whole is consecrated through special feasts and seasons. Of these the most important are the Lenten-Easter season with its feasts of Easter and Pentecost and the Advent-Christmas season with its feasts of Christmas and Epiphany. These seasons celebrate the great events of Christian redemption and make present again to believing Christians the riches of the Lord's power and merits (SC 107, 102).

The liturgy of the hours also is a model for a truly Christian manner of worship. Praise of God, prayer and scriptural instruction are the heart of a fully Catholic worship. The praise of God is especially expressed through the psalms, prayed in the traditional Christian way as fulfilled in Christ, supplemented by hymns and songs that are scriptural in inspiration (SC 24, GILH 100). Scripture itself is read regularly in a way that both supports the Liturgical Year and provides a review of Christian teaching and of the scripture itself understood in the light of the traditional interpretation of the Fathers. Scripture, indeed, is of paramount importance in the celebration of the liturgy and therefore of all of Christian prayer (SC 24, DV 21). Those who are not able to use the full liturgy of the hours can follow a similar approach and can draw upon the sequence of psalms and canticles and the cycles of readings it offers.

Those who belong to covenant communities should live lives of daily prayer in various ways. The community itself should worship God together as the center of its life, sometimes by celebrating the liturgy. When possible, the different groupings within the community who live together, the families and households of single people, should worship the Lord morning and evening in a way modeled by the liturgy of the hours. Each member likewise should pray individually (SC 12). Moreover, the whole community should read, study and meditate upon the scriptures and other Christian teaching in order to follow the Lord more fully and to observe the Christian seasons. While the patterns of life differ according to the call and spirituality of the community and according to the relationship it has to the Church as a whole, the spiritual life is one, based on the same truth and shaped by the spirit of the same liturgy.

3. COVENANT COMMUNITY AND SACRAMENTS

The sacraments are signs and means through which Christ acts in and through his Church to sanctify his disciples, to build up his body and to give worship to God his Father (SC 59, CIC, Can 840). The life of the covenant community is therefore dependent upon the sacraments and nourished by them, whether these sacraments are performed within the life of the community itself or whether its members receive them in parishes or other contexts outside the covenant community.

Renewal of the liturgical life of the Catholic Church involves a renewal in the celebration of the sacraments and in the way they are approached by Christ's faithful. The renewal is brought to completion in the lives of Christians when the sacraments perform the role for which they were instituted. The sacraments are central to the Christian life, and this centrality is primarily made effective by receiving them in a way which strengthens that life. The sacraments are closely connected to everything foundational in the Christian life, because they unite us to Christ and make effective his action of transforming us in him. They do not, however, function in a foundational way by becoming themselves the center of focus. Rather as signs they should reveal Christ and his action in us.

The source and ongoing foundation of a renewed use of the sacraments is a renewed faith and conversion (SC 11, CIC, Can 836). Those who receive sacraments in a life-giving way have faith in Christ. They especially have faith in his active presence in their lives, including faith that he will act through the sacraments they receive. They have been converted to Christ as their Master and Lord and are therefore desirous of following him and obeying him. That conversion leads to the proper response to each sacrament. Those who receive the sacraments well are instructed in Christian truth. They understand the meaning of the signs themselves in such a way that they can participate in each sacramental celebration fully, consciously, and actively, responding to the Lord in a fitting way (SC 14).

For most that concerns sacraments there is no difference between the life of covenant communities and that of the rest of the Church. The sacraments, however, are celebrations of the Church itself as the "sacrament of unity," that is, the holy people united and ordered under the bishops (CIC, Can 837). Through the sacraments the sacred nature and organic structure of the priestly community is brought into operation (LG 11). They establish, strengthen and manifest ecclesiastical communion (CIC, Can 840). Therefore the approach to the sacraments in covenant communities touches at various points upon the relationship of the covenant community to the Church and likewise can affect the way in which the members of the community participate in sacramental actions. Such points call for special concern on the part of the leaders of covenant communities.

4. THE EUCHARISTIC ASSEMBLY

The Eucharistic assembly is central to the corporate life of the Church because by means of it the unity of God's people is signified and brought about, and the building up of the body of Christ is perfected (CIC, Can 897). At the heart of the assembly is the Eucharistic Sacrifice of the body and blood of the Lord, instituted to perpetuate the sacrifice of the cross and to give to the Church a memorial of his death and resurrection. It is a sacrament of love, a sign of unity, a bond of charity, a paschal banquet in which Christ is consumed, the mind is filled with grace, and a pledge of future glory is given to us (SC 47).

The main assembly of the covenant community can sometimes be a Sunday Eucharistic assembly. Normally, however, for pastoral reasons the community assembly cannot be the regular place of liturgical celebration for its members on Sunday. In such situations, the life of the community should prepare its members to value and seek participation in a full Eucharistic celebration on the Lord's Day.

The covenant community may be able to supplement the Sunday Eucharistic celebration by an additional celebration of the Eucharist during the week for the whole community or for sections of the community. It may also be able to provide a daily Eucharistic celebration for some members of the community or to encourage attendance at a common Eucharistic celebration outside the community. These various ways of increasing Eucharistic participation should be approached in ways that do not distort the shape of the liturgical life of the Church.

An additional celebration of the Eucharist during the week for the whole community should not take precedence in the lives of its members over the celebrations of the whole Church on the Lord's Day. Sunday is the original feast day, the foundation and nucleus of the whole liturgical year (SC 106). Encouraging the daily attendance of some community members at a Eucharistic celebration should not lead to approaching the Eucharist as an individual devotion or source of individual strengthening rather than as a communal celebration of the Church (SC 26). The Eucharist is the one bread that makes many one body (1 Co 11:17). Nor should it lead to the Eucharistic Sacrifice being celebrated primarily for the convenience of the individual rather than with due honor as an act of the worship of the divine majesty (SC 33), the full public worship of the mystical body of Christ (SC 7).

Finally, appreciation for the Eucharist, often coupled with evangelistic zeal, should not lead to celebrations of the Eucharist which encourage many to participate and take communion who are not properly prepared and so fail in respect for the holiness of the body and blood of the Lord (1 Co 11:27-32). The Eucharistic celebration is to be so ordered that all the participants derive from it the many fruits for which Christ the Lord instituted the Eucharistic Sacrifice (CIC, Can 895).

5. THE SACRAMENTS OF INITIATION

The sacraments of Christian initiation are the beginning of the Christian life, in that they complete our union with Christ. Through them we can be said to have put on Christ and be made one body in him (Gal 3:27, 1 Co 12:13, AG 14, LG 14). Since the baptism of children has a family orientation, it can be celebrated as an expression of the life of the covenant community even when it is performed in a parochial context. The further sacramental steps in the initiation of children, first communion and confirmation, will be approached in various ways depending on how the covenant community is related to the structures of the Church. Commonly it will be helpful for the covenant community to have a program of Christian conversion and growth for the children who are members of the community, even when they attend religious instruction in parishes. Such programs could contain preparation for the sacramental steps of initiation where pastorally practical and helpful. They can also form children of community members in the spirituality of the community (CIC, Can 214).

As renewal communities, covenant communities bring their members to a new conversion to Christ, even those who have already received full sacramental initiation into the Catholic Church and are living a Christian life. Conversion should lead to a full living of the Christian life, whether for the first time or as an increase of what was already present.

Without attempting to repeat the sacraments of initiation, the program of conversion and formation in the covenant community should be patterned upon the adult catechumenate traditional in the first centuries of Christianity and renewed in our day. It therefore should include a renewal of the faith commitment of baptism and a release or strengthening of the presence and action of the Holy Spirit. In addition, it should include a formation period for the whole Christian life that should lead to the true following of Christ appropriate to disciples (AG 14).

For those who have not previously been Christians or have not completed their full sacramental initiation into the Church, the formation into covenant community membership can also be a time in which their Christian initiation is completed. Much of that initiation can be provided by the program of community formation since what is needed for entry into the Christian life is much the same as what is needed for coming into a renewed Christian life. The way we receive Christ provides the pattern of renewal of our life in him (Col 2:6).

6. THE SACRAMENT OF PENANCE

The sacrament of penance provides from God through the absolution of a lawful minister the forgiveness of sins committed after baptism. It likewise provides reconciliation with the Church (CIC, Can 959). Even as the sacraments of initiation complete the process of initiation, so the sacrament of penance completes the process of repentance or penance by which the individuals are brought to a recognition of wrongdoing and to a decision to repudiate it and to amend their lives (CIC, Can 987). Much of what is needed for an understanding of the relationship of the covenant community to the broader Church in regard to the sacrament of penance is contained in section II, 3 above.

The renewal of the sacrament of penance has to include a renewal in the primary purpose of the sacrament. While the confession of venial sins and of imperfections is helpful, the sacrament of penance is primarily instituted for the forgiveness of grave sins (CIC, Can 988). In order to support the proper use of the sacrament in regard to grave sin, the recognition of the objective seriousness of grave sins should be fostered in the life of the covenant community, and community support and discipline should call those who have fallen back to a life of Christian righteousness and strengthen them in it.

Repentance or penance goes beyond turning away from or repairing grave sins to a positive growth in holiness. This growth in the completeness of love that constitutes holiness involves leaving behind unloving ways. Here the ongoing support of those who desire to live a deeper Christian life is a source of great help.

Many covenant communities provide methods of review of life for their members which help them to live lives free of sin and encourage them to greater holiness. The devotional use of the sacrament of penance, whether within the community context or outside of it, can also be a means of spiritual strengthening in the process of growth in holiness. It can especially be so when joined to a communal life that fosters holiness of life. In a renewed Christian life we can be dead to sin and alive to God in Christ Jesus, walking according to the Spirit (Ro 6:11, 8:5).

7. MARRIAGE

The marriage covenant is the means by which a man and a woman establish between themselves a partnership of their whole life, one that is ordered of its very nature to the well-being of the spouses and to the procreation and the bringing up of children (CIC, Can 1055). The covenant community can be a powerful support to marriage and family life as to other aspects of Christian living (CIC, Can 1063).

The covenant community can either provide the marriage instruction in accordance with the norms of the local church or can provide supplementary instruction. Such instruction can not only strengthen the couples' awareness of the nature of Christian marriage and of the roles and objectives of Christian spouses and parents (CIC, Can 1003), but also instruct them in the community support for their courtship and marriage. It can thereby help them integrate their married life more effectively into the corporate life of the community as well as of the broader church.

The marriage ceremony itself, because of its family orientation, is naturally an expression of the life of the community when those being married are both community members, even though the marriage is normally celebrated in a parochial context. Where the celebration of the marriage is largely formed by community members, the marriage ceremony should be Christ-centered. It should bring to full expression the way in which the couple is establishing a cell of the body of Christ, committing themselves in faithfulness to a life of Christian discipleship together and modeling themselves on Christ and the Church (CIC, Can 1063).

Since the marriage ceremony frequently provides an occasion for bringing nonbelievers or nominal Christians to a Christian service, it should be conducted with evangelistic sensitivity and in a way that does not encourage the reception of communion by those who should not do so. Since the marriage ceremony also frequently provides an occasion for Christians of another church or ecclesial community to attend a Catholic service, it should be conducted with ecumenical sensitivity showing an added concern to see that there is a balanced expression of Christian truth which avoids leading others into error regarding the true doctrine of the Church (UR 11, LG 67). Most importantly, the celebration of the sacrament of marriage should be a witness to the reality of Christ and the blessing for family life which comes from following him.

8. CONCLUSION

The purpose of the sacraments is to sanctify human beings, to build up the body of Christ and to give worship to God (SC 59). Participation in sacramental life should first of all lead to a growth in holiness in the members of the covenant community wherever they participate in it, whether within the context of covenant community life or in other situations. Celebration of the sacraments should also lead to a building up of the body of Christ. It should strengthen the life of covenant community when celebrated within that covenant community. At the same time it should strengthen the life of the whole Church. The greater good of the Church as a whole, in fact, provides the guidance for when and how sacraments should be celebrated within the life of the covenant community. Finally, sacraments should be celebrated in a way in which God is truly worshiped so that their very celebration honors him and reveals his glory to the human race.

Afterword

THE PLAN OF GOD is corporate. This can be seen in the way God, the source of all good, "created man in his own image and likeness...male and female he created them" (Gen 1:27). This can also be seen in the vision of the new Jerusalem which God, the end of all worthwhile human endeavor, will bring about at the ordained time. The new Jerusalem will be a city of mutual love in which God will dwell with his people (Rev 21:3-4). Each person will know God as Father and one another as brothers and sisters and fellow servants.

Covenant communities have come into existence to allow many of Christ's faithful to live a life of discipleship more fully. Because they seek to do this together, members of covenant communities seek to achieve God's original purpose for the human race as fully as they can in this fallen world. In doing so they begin to live in this age the life of the age to come. "The Spirit and the Bride say, 'Come.' Amen. Come, Lord Jesus!" (Rev 22:17, 20).

Part Two

*A Selection
of Documents*

Introduction

THE FOLLOWING IS A SELECTION of documents that have been influential in the development of covenant communities in the Catholic Church. I have chosen them because of their historic importance. In my experience, these are the documents which most encouraged and shaped the covenant community movement. Others perhaps could have, but I believe that these were the ones that did. Perhaps someone else would come up with a different selection.

First, I have included excerpts from two documents put out by the U.S. Catholic bishops. These turned out to be especially important since both the Catholic charismatic renewal and Catholic covenant communities began in the United States, and the stance of encouragement that the U.S. bishops took towards both became a model for other bishops. A full collection of hierarchical statements on the charismatic renewal can be found in the collection *Presence, Power, Praise* edited by Kilian McDonnell, OSB (Collegeville Liturgical Press, 1980).

I have also included lengthy excerpts from two documents published in 1978, the Malines document *Ecumenism and the Charismatic Renewal* by Cardinal Suenens and *The Charismatic Renewal and Ecumenism* by Kilian McDonnell, OSB. The Malines documents were a series published by Cardinal Suenens to provide theological-pastoral foundation and orientation for the charismatic renewal. The earliest of these were cooperative efforts by teams of scholars and consultants. The one on ecumenism turned out to be particularly important for the development of covenant communities, because it of necessity focused on the relationship of covenant communities to Church and hierarchy. In my recollection, these were the discussions that led to the fellowship model* for ecumenical communities, later accepted by some diocesan bishops and recognized by the Council for the laity. More importantly, they led to what we would now speak about as the lay association model for covenant communities.

Out of the Malines discussion on ecumenism came not only the second Malines document, but also Fr. McDonnell's work. I have excerpts from both, because both provided helpful direction for the development of covenant communities.

I have, in addition, included some excerpts from recent documents from the universal Church on lay associations. Covenant communities are by no means the only lay associations in the Church. However, to the best of my knowledge all the covenant communities and Catholic fellowships in ecumenical communities with hierarchical approval have been approved as lay associations.

The excerpts I have included contain the juridical grounding for their existence, especially the development of the "right of association."

The right of association was clearly stated in the Decree on the Lay Apostolate and is recognized now for the first time explicitly in canon law. It has, however, been the basis of renewal movements in the Church from the earliest centuries, as I sketched in my book *Unordained Elders and Renewal Communities*, (Paramus, NJ, Paulist, 1976). It was the basis, as well, for the development of covenant communities with the

---

* The statutes of the Catholic Fraternity of Covenant Communities and Fellowships, approved by the International Council for the Laity defines "fellowships" as follows: (8) 'Fellowship' is a term that describes a constituted group of Catholics who live a covenant community lifestyle and maintain a bond of charity, prayer and witness with Christians or groups of Christians belonging to other confessions within a broader ecumenical community.

encouragement of many bishops and Vatican officials in the years between Vatican Council II and the publication of the revised Code of Canon Law in 1983.

Finally, I am including an excerpt from a memorandum sent by Jacques Maritain to Pope Paul VI in 1965 and published posthumously. Maritain's memorandum and the thinking behind it has been influential in modern Catholic development. He lays his finger upon a key theological understanding for explaining the existence of covenant communities in the modern Church. For the most part, covenant communities came from a renewal in the appreciation of the spiritual mission of the laity. In retrospect, I believe it is possible to see that it is precisely this understanding that allowed the development of the Catholic charismatic renewal as a renewal movement and the covenant communities as approved renewal communities.

A Selection of Documents

SELECTION ONE

From *Catholic Charismatic Renewal*, the National Conference of Catholic Bishops, (Washington, USCC, 1975, p.6):

14. A more recent development in the renewal is the establishment of small communities in which members of the movement live together in order to deepen their life in the Spirit. The success of these communities depends on mature leadership, on careful fidelity to the norms mentioned in the earlier part of this paper and on a strong link with the ecclesial community. Regular and objective evaluation with outside help is very important. In his closing address to the World Synod of Bishops on October 26, 1974, the Holy Father encouraged the development of small communities but called for a sense of balance: "In addition we have noted with satisfaction the hope furnished by small communities and the reminder they give of the work of the Holy Spirit. But this hope would be truly stunted if their ecclesial life, in the organic unity of the single Body of Christ, were to cease or be exempted

from legitimate ecclesiastical authority or be left to the arbitrary impulse of individuals."

SELECTION TWO

From *A Pastoral Statement on the Catholic Charismatic Renewal*, National Conference of Catholic Bishops (Washington, D.C. 1989, pp. 6-9, 13-14):

Mature Lay Life

8. The charismatic renewal is a movement which seeks to be completely open to the Holy Spirit as it contributes to the ongoing effort to renew the whole Church. Though the Catholic charismatic renewal has influenced many bishops, priests and religious personally, it has contributed in an even more profound way to the realization of the role of the laity in the mission of the Church. From its beginning on university campuses, to the formation of thousands of parish prayer groups, it has been largely led, taught, discerned and participated in by lay people. In a way not known in recent history, lay men and women are engaged in evangelization and the proclamation of the Lordship of Jesus, in programs of spiritual formation and spiritual direction. Clearly the charismatic renewal has as its goal the transformation of all the members of the People of God.

Community and the Credibility of the Gospel

11. If some people judge that God is no longer relevant to their lives, one reason is the lack of a vital Christian community in which they can experience his presence and power and can see and hear the Gospel preached and lived authentically. The charismatic renewal has grasped the communitarian dimension of the Good News. The return to different forms of community is prompted by the deepest Christian instinct. The first reaction of the early Church to the presence of the risen Christ and the

power of the Spirit was the formation of community, which constituted the historic nucleus of Church (Ac 2:44-47, 4:32-35). Within the context of today's Church, committed Christians have come together to find spiritual nourishment, to pray and praise, to evangelize, to serve others. A variety of communities arise in this way. There are inter-parochial prayer groups, parish prayer groups and covenant communities. Some are wholly Catholic in membership; some are ecumenical. In all of the various community forms there is evidence of a great spiritual hunger for God, his presence and his Word.

Covenant Communities

13. The emergence of covenant communities is a development of major importance. By providing leadership resources, formation programs, growth seminars, and sharing across a large spectrum of human and spiritual needs, they have become a significant sign of the kingdom of God present in power. Every state and stage of life is there represented: married, single, widowed, old and young. Through collaboration with the local bishop, these communities have developed new approaches to the pursuit of full Catholic life.

14. Within some of these covenant communities are households of men and households of women who are "single for the Lord," that is, living a life of committed celibacy, evangelical simplicity and poverty, developing profoundly human and graced bonds of friendship and fellowship, which make these celibate communities effective tools of evangelization, especially among the youth. Some of these brotherhoods and sisterhoods, existing within the structure of a covenant community, have an ecumenical character.

Ecumenism

22. We see in the charismatic renewal an ecumenical force in which we rejoice. We make our own the words of Pope

Paul VI, repeated by Pope John Paul II during his visit to the United States (October 5, 1979): "Let the work of drawing near to our separated brethren go on, with much understanding, with much patience, with great love; but without deviating from the true Catholic doctrine." Included in this are a balance between Word and sacraments as channels of grace; the recognition of the liturgy as the "indispensable source of the true Christian spirit"; traditional devotion to Mary the Mother of God; and our obedience to the Holy Father, the successor of St. Peter. Authentic ecumenism maintains loyalty to the life and broad experience of the Church.

SELECTION THREE

From *Ecumenism and Charismatic Renewal*, Malines Document 2, by Leon Joseph Cardinal Suenens, (Ann Arbor: Servant, 1978, pp. 85-88):

Ecumenical Communities

Communities involve a greater degree of commitment and participation than prayer groups. Hence they raise further issues.

In the circumstance, it is useful to distinguish between the prayer groups which the Charismatic Renewal is engendering throughout the world and the "Christian life communities" which are springing up in many areas.

Within the Charismatic Renewal, "Christian community" is a term that designates a group of Christians living in a particular area, who have committed themselves to support one another in their Christian life. The way in which this support is expressed may vary depending on local circumstances and on the nature of the commitment, but such communities come together regularly for worship and for other activities that promote a common life.

Communities are composed of married couples, single

people, and children; some communities include men and women who are "single for the Lord," that is, who have consecrated themselves to the Lord's service, either for life or for some shorter specified period.

Members of communities may or may not live together in "households"—residential units usually composed of a married couple and several single people, of single men, or of single women. They may or may not hold their money and possessions in common.

Some of these communities are interdenominational: open to members of various Church bodies on an equal basis. Others are denominational; designed to be especially at the service of members of one Church body, while remaining open to Christians from other traditions. Whatever the emphasis, both types of communities are concerned with ecumenism.

1. *General Guidelines for Ecumenical Communities*

Here, therefore, are a few principles for pastoral guidance which need amplification to meet local situations.

a. *Consultation with Church Authorities*—The participation of Catholics in an ecumenical community must be carefully determined by previous consultation with the local bishop or with the National Ecumenical Commission set up by the Catholic hierarchy. As stated in a document issued in 1975 by the Vatican Secretariat for Promoting Christian Unity:

> Where joint actions or programs are decided on, they ought to be undertaken fully by both sides and duly authorized by the respective authorities right from the earliest stages of planning.

> Catholic life and involvement in the ecumenical community should also have the approval of the local bishop.

b. *Proper Formation for Catholic Members*—The guidelines concerning a solid Catholic formation for Catholics in ecumenical prayer groups apply equally to Catholics in ecumenical communities. Here too, it is necessary to fulfill, in a balanced and harmonious fashion, all the requirements that enable the specific character of the Catholic members, and their fidelity to genuine ecumenism, to be wholly respected.

c. *Problems Involving Individual Community Members*—When organizational problems arise in the life of a community member, these principles should be followed:

—Problems dealing with involvement in the Church should be resolved directly with the leaders of the church body, as members of the Church, and not from the standpoint of membership of the community.
—Problems dealing with involvement in the community should be resolved with the leaders of the community.
—In situations where there is an overlapping concern about the same individual or group of individuals, there should be communication between the pastors of the church bodies and the leaders of the communities (presuming that these are not the same persons).

d. *Problems Involving Catholic Doctrine*—Whenever a problem touching upon the Catholic doctrine of ecumenical practice arises, the appropriate Catholic episcopal authority is the final adjudicator. The Catholic leadership of the community should be in adequate communication and unity with that authority.

2. *The Need for Further Study*

Pastoral guidance in the sphere of ecumenism is a new and delicate matter. In some respects, it reminds us of the pastoral problems connected with mixed marriages, although in the latter case the official rulings concern men and women who are "separated" in doctrine but "united" by virtue of the marriage bond. It is heartening to report that at the present moment research into the question of mixed marriages is being carried out with the full collaboration of the official authorities.

Likewise under study is the problem of how to do full justice to the ecumenical experience in Christian communities. For Catholics who feel called to this type of ecumenical community life, the most viable formula would doubtless be the setting up of a "Catholic fraternity" or "fellowship" within the larger community; its links and modes of relationship with the ecumenical community, reviewed on a pluralist basis, would have to be clearly defined.

This type of structure is now being examined, in collaboration with the competent authorities, by "The Word of God," a community in Ann Arbor (Michigan, U.S.A.), which is attracting world-wide attention through its influence and breadth of vision. Parallel researches are being pursued within the framework of other major confessions.

Once all the requirements of the religious identity proper to each church body have been acknowledged, the modalities of holding and sharing things in common will grow out of experience. So let us place our trust in the Holy Spirit and in the good will of all Christians to the cause of unity.

SELECTION FOUR

From *The Charismatic Renewal and Ecumenism,* by Kilian McDonnell, OSB, (Ann Arbor: Servant, 1978, pp. 79-80, 95-105, 111-112):

The Non-Denominational and the Ecumenical

A related question is that of the difference between non-denominational and ecumenical. Both describe how Protestants, Anglicans, Orthodox and Roman Catholics come together in meetings, prayer groups and covenant communities, and each of these groups can, in its proper way, be a fact of unity which the Spirit himself has created. In brief, non-denominational events are those in which persons come together across denominational lines on the basis of their common faith in Jesus as Lord, setting aside those areas in which there is disagreement between Protestants and Catholics. Non-denominational meetings are based solely on areas of agreement. Ecumenical events, on the other hand, are those in which persons come together across denominational lines on the basis both of their common faith in Jesus and of their lack of complete unity in faith. Both areas of agreement and disagreement typify the ecumenical meeting or event. Each of these two approaches should be evaluated positively and each as circumstances in which the one is to be preferred to the other.

This is not to say that every person who is involved in some Protestant-Catholic activity must consciously decide whether that involvement is to be ecumenical or nondenominational. Most persons come together across denominational lines to share a common faith in Jesus who is Lord, to praise that Lordship and to give a common witness. They are together for a purpose on which they can agree without consciousness of the specific character of their gathering. In a real sense they do not come together specifically to further the purposes of the ecumenical movement, though these gatherings do advance the movement toward the unity of the churches. But that advance is a by-product, a very real and desirable one, but a by-product, nonetheless. One does not have in these gatherings a dialogue situation, clearly ecumenical, which exists when two or more churches come together in an official way with professionally competent theologians to study areas of agreement and disagreement. In this kind of dialogue ecumenism, the unity of the churches, is not a by-product but the main purpose of the gathering.

While it is not necessary that each participant be conscious of the specific character of every event, it should be clear in the minds of those who are involved in the planning. As a general norm, national, regional and local meetings should be ecumenical in character. Nonetheless, there are particular circumstances where such meetings might more properly be non-denominational. There might be specific meetings where careful planning would combine non-denominational and ecumenical elements. But the dominant character of the overall way in which Protestants, Anglicans, Orthodox and Roman Catholics relate to one another should be ecumenical rather than non-denominational.

In prayer meetings, covenant communities and households there can be both non-denominational and ecumenical expressions of their common life. In order to avoid a vague churchless Christianity, there should be some visible (or audible) expression of what divides the churches. Leaders of ecumenical communities need to have great ecumenical sensitivity so that the members retain their religious identity. Persons, whether Protestant or Catholic, who do not have a truly ecumenical commitment and understanding should not be leaders. Catholic leaders no less than others should have an ecumenical attitude and should safeguard the integrity of Protestant members. Those who embrace an exclusively non-denominational stance should not assume leadership positions.

Ecclesial Ambiguity of Ecumenical Groups
At the theological level there is an ambiguity in the situation of ecumenical prayer groups and communities. The communion in the life from the Father to the Father, which is the primary fact of the Church's life, is not a matter of an abstract disembodied fellowship. An international group of ecumenists pointed to the pragmatic necessities implied here: "The communion with God which we receive

by grace is always realized in the concrete form of Christ's Church." No concrete expression of communion is possible apart from the Church.

Where two to three are gathered together in the name of Christ across denominational lines, a small community is formed: this smallest of communities has some ecclesial significance. Evidently it is related in some way to that people of God (1 Pet 2:9, 10), to the spouse (2 Co 11:2), to the flock of whom Christ is the Good Shepherd (Jn 10:11), and to that gathering which is the body of Christ (2 Co 12:12), the Church. Though related to and in some degree manifesting that manifold mystery of the Church, the local ecumenical prayer groups and communities by themselves are not the local Church. "The first Pentecostals as described in Acts were surely not just an enthusiastic prayer group but the community of the Risen Lord...Genuine Christianity was ecclesial from the beginning." This does not mean that they must be absorbed by the local parish. The parish is not the only permissible form of the local Church. One thinks immediately of convents and monasteries which certainly are "Church," though they are not the local parish, though their members may never attend the local parish. Ecumenical prayer groups and covenant communities do have an ecclesial (Church) character, yet they are not the local Church, partly because in the present discipline they cannot be Eucharistic communities, which convents and monasteries can. The communion in the life from the Father to the Father is realized in the concrete form of the Church which celebrates the Eucharist. One sees clearly the ambiguity of these ecumenical groups: They are ecclesial (have a relation to the mystery of the Church) but they are not the local Church partly because they cannot be Eucharistic.

Unless the ambiguity of ecumenical communities is kept in mind, they will develop into another stream of Christianity, neither Orthodox, Protestant, Catholic,

Anglican nor classical Pentecostal, but a vague enthusiastic melange of churchless Christianity. Rather than contribute to the unity of the churches, it would constitute another obstacle, another division within Christianity and would deprive the churches of the most important unitive force on the ecumenical scene today.

Not all communities within the renewal have or should have broad ecumenical participation. Much will depend on circumstance. But where they exist they can be a witness to the credibility of the gospel. In addition, they fulfill the function of presenting the churches with new creative models for future ecumenical developments. This they do both in the manner in which they relate to one another under their common Lord, and in the mutual respect for each other's religious heritage. In a unique way they present models of Christians coming together in a communion of praise and thanksgiving.

From *Pastoral Suggestions* (pp. 99-105):
4. In the most fervent communities, there is broad ecumenical sharing along a whole spectrum: faith in a common Lord, prayer, witness, living quarters, meals and finances. The children are often brought up in a deep personal knowledge of Jesus and a profound commitment of the Christian life but are wanting, for instance, in a knowledge of the sacraments. Some periods of instruction should be part of the yearly schedule in which Catholics can learn the full riches of their faith and develop a Catholic sense. The same initiation into their respective identities should be provided for Protestants, Anglicans and Orthodox.

5. There is nothing in the renewal that makes it necessarily sectarian. Yet it must be recognized that unless the full Catholic doctrine and experience are imparted to members of prayer groups and covenant communities, these may become isolated from the life of the Church and

can become sectarian. Therefore, there should be occasions when teaching is given in these areas of the Catholic faith in which our separated brethren are not in agreement. This can be done in various ways, certain times during days of renewal or in workshops in regional conferences, or in days set aside in groups of households. The same opportunities should be given to Protestant members regarding the riches of their own faith.

Expressing Ecumenicity Within Catholicity
19. In ecumenical prayer groups and covenant communities there should be community expression which articulates both the groups' Catholicity and their ecumenicity. Catholics take it for granted that these are not two unrelated streams. Rather, their ecumenicity is an expression of their Catholicity. Persons share prayer and witness, for instance, as expressions of their unity in Christ, of their ecumenicity. There should be community expressions of their dividedness. This can be painful for all concerned but unless this pain is faced and honored, all will become comfortable with the scandal of division and nothing will happen. Ecumenical pain should neither be dismissed nor ignored.

To give expression to their lack of complete unity, the Catholic members could celebrate the Eucharist separately three or four times a year, not necessarily as a part of the weekly prayer meeting. (It is self understood that Catholics are attending Sunday Mass in their parishes.) The Orthodox, Lutheran and Anglican members could do the same. Further, occasionally the Catholics could have a communal penance service. When Catholics in the prayer group or covenant community predominate, especially when this is by a large percentage, all of this should be done in a non-threatening way. There would be less ecumenical tension if the Catholic leaders would demonstrate by their occasional attendance at weekday Mass that the Eucharistic life is simply a part of their mature Catholic faith. Unless there is this commitment, both to full Catholicity and to full ecumenicity, the communities will, perhaps quite unconsciously, develop into a vague non-denominational pattern.

Pastoral Suggestions

20. Ecumenical groups can make a contribution to the unity of the Church and such groups should be evaluated positively. There may be circumstances which make it advisable that groups in certain areas be exclusively Protestant or exclusively Catholic. As long as such groups are not triumphantly sectarian, their non-ecumenical membership should not be immediately interpreted as being anti-ecumenical.

21. Groups which do not have mature leadership should not attempt to become ecumenical. Nor should every prayer group feel that it has a call to be an ecumenical covenant community.

From the Epilogue (pp. 111-112):

Two great styles of approaching the division of the churches exist, both necessary for ecumenical success. First, formal dialogues involving trained theologians attempt to resolve the important doctrinal differences so that the walls which divide and render full communion and fellowship impossible can be removed. The dialogue way begins with doctrine. No doubt should be raised as to the continuing importance of this style of ecumenical work.

Another style, which the charismatic renewal and other groups in the Church represent, starts at the other end. They begin in love and sharing. On the basis of the communion they already share, they build fellowships of love and commitment. This is the family reconciliation spoken of earlier, where alienated brothers and sister reunite in love to the point where they are willing to lay down their lives for one another. This is no mere metaphor. The bond covers the whole spectrum of human relationships and is so deep that the remaining doctrinal differences are approached with a different perspective. In this style the depth of shared fellowship does not make doctrinal differences evaporate. But the profound sharing makes it possible to approach the doctrinal differences with a new theological and spiritual discernment. In this style one begins with a communion so sacrificial and self-forgetful that the truth of the gospel is more quickly grasped and the doctrinal barriers to full fellowship are more easily removed.

One of the contributions of the charismatic renewal to the reunion of the churches is this ecumenism of family reconciliation which begins with fellowship in Christ. Only the unperceptive would dismiss this ecumenical force as ephemeral enthusiasm. On the contrary the charismatic renewal is the single most potent force for the ecumenical scene today. And it is here to stay. Both it and its ecumenical significance are permanent elements in the life of the Roman Catholic Church.

Great hopes are entertained that the unity willed for the Church by the Lord will prevail and be realized. It is a hope, however, without illusions. Though what unites is greater than what divides, one is still faced with a situation in which there is both substantial unity and substantial disunity, a situation which is a scandal to the world to which the Church is sent.

The Catholic charismatic renewal wishes to live at the center of that communion which is the Church, and desires to be a part of that impulse of the Spirit which removes the public scandal, restores the fullness of unity and leads all back to the Father.

SELECTION FIVE

From *The Code of Canon Law,* (The Canon Law Society of America, 1983, pp. 70-77, 104-109, 114-115):

> Can. 208 In virtue of their rebirth in Christ there exists among all the Christian faithful a true equality with regard to dignity and the activity whereby all cooperate in the building up of the Body of Christ in accord with each one's own condition and function.
>
> Can. 209 §1. The Christian faithful are bound by an obligation, even in their own patterns of activity, always to maintain communion with the Church.
>
> §2. They are to fulfill with great diligence the duties which they owe to the universal Church and to the particular Church to which they belong according to the prescriptions of law.
>
> Can. 210 All the Christian faithful must make an effort, in accord with their own condition, to live a holy life and to promote the growth of the Church and its continual sanctification.
>
> Can. 211 All the Christian faithful have the duty and the right to work so that the divine message of salvation may increasingly reach the whole of humankind in every age and in every land.
>
> Can. 214 The Christian faithful have the right to worship God according to the prescriptions of their own rite approved by the legitimate pastors of the Church, and to follow their own form of spiritual life consonant with the teaching of the Church.
>
> Can. 215 The Christian faithful are at liberty freely to found and to govern associations for charitable and religious purposes or for the promotion of the Christian vocation in the world; they are free to hold meetings to pursue these purposes in common.

Can. 216 All the Christian faithful, since they participate in the mission of the Church, have the right to promote or to sustain apostolic action by their own undertakings in accord with each one's state and condition; however, no undertaking shall assume the name Catholic unless the consent of competent ecclesiastical authority is given.

Can. 223 §1. In exercising their rights the Christian faithful, both as individuals and when gathered in associations, must take account of the common good of the Church and of the rights of others as well as their own duties toward others.

§2. In the interest of the common good, ecclesiastical authority has competence to regulate the exercise of the rights which belong to the Christian faithful.

Can. 225 §1. Since the laity, like all the Christian faithful, are deputed by God to the apostolate through their baptism and confirmation, they are therefore bound by the general obligations and enjoy the general right to work as individuals or in associations so that the divine message of salvation becomes known and accepted by all persons throughout the world; this obligation has a greater impelling force in those circumstances in which people can hear the gospel and know Christ only through lay persons.

§2. Each lay person in accord with his or her condition is bound by a special duty to imbue and perfect the order of temporal affairs with the spirit of the gospel; they thus give witness to Christ in a special way in carrying out those affairs and in exercising secular duties.

Can. 226 §1. Lay persons who live in the married state in accord with their own vocation are bound by a special duty to work for the upbuilding of the people of God through their marriage and their family.

§2. Because they have given life to their children, parents have a most serious obligation and enjoy the right to educate them; therefore Christian parents are especially to care for the Christian education of their children according to the teaching handed on by the Church.

Can. 227 Lay Christian faithful have the right to have recognized that freedom in the affairs of the earthly city which belongs to all citizens; when they exercise such freedom, however, they are to take care that their actions are imbued with the spirit of the gospel and take into account the doctrine set forth by the magisterium of the Church; but they are to avoid proposing their own opinion as the teaching of the Church in questions which are open to various opinions.

Can. 298 §1. In the Church there are associations distinct from institutes of consecrated life and societies of apostolic life, in which the Christian faithful, either clergy or laity, or clergy and laity together, strive by common effort to promote a more perfect life or to foster public worship or Christian doctrine or to exercise other apostolic works, namely to engage in efforts of evangelization, to exercise works of piety or charity and to animate the temporal order with the Christian spirit.

§2. The Christian faithful should enroll especially in associations which are erected or praised or recommended by competent ecclesiastical authority.

Can. 299 §1. The Christian faithful are free, by means of a private agreement made among themselves, to establish associations to attain the aims mentioned in can. 298, §1., with due regard for the prescriptions of can. 301, §1.

§2. Such associations are called private associations even though they are praised or recommended by ecclesiastical authority.

§3. No private association of the Christian faithful in the Church is recognized unless its statutes are reviewed by competent authority.

Can. 300 No association shall assume the name "Catholic" without the consent of competent ecclesiastical authority, in accord with the norm of can. 312.

Can. 301 §1. Competent ecclesiastical authority alone has the right to erect associations of the Christian faithful which set out to teach Christian doctrine in the name of the Church or to promote public worship or which aim at other ends whose pursuit by their nature is reserved to the same ecclesiastical authority.

§2. Competent ecclesiastical authority, if it judges it expedient, can also erect associations of the Christian faithful in order to attain directly or indirectly other spiritual ends whose accomplishment has not been sufficiently provided for by the efforts of private persons.

§3. Associations of the Christian faithful which are erected by competent ecclesiastical authority are called public associations.

Can. 305 §1. All associations of the Christian faithful are subject to the vigilance of competent ecclesiastical authority, whose duty it is to take care that integrity of faith and morals is preserved in them and to watch lest abuse creep into ecclesiastical discipline; therefore that authority has the right and duty to visit them in accord with the norm of law and the statutes; such associations are also subject to the governance of the same authority according to the prescriptions of the following canons.

§2. Associations of any kind whatever are subject to the vigilance of the Holy See; diocesan associations and also other associations to the extent that they work in the diocese are subject to the vigilance of the local ordinary.

Can. 321 The Christian faithful guide and direct private associations according to the prescripts of their statutes.

Can. 322 §1. A private association of the Christian faithful can acquire juridic personality by means of a formal decree of the competent ecclesiastical authority mentioned in can. 312.

§2. No private association of the Christian faithful can acquire juridic personality unless its statutes have been approved by the ecclesiastical authority mentioned in can. 312, §1; however, the approval of the statute does not change the private nature of the association.

Can. 323 §1. Although private associations of the Christian faithful enjoy autonomy in accord with the norm of can. 312, they are subject to the vigilance of ecclesiastical authority in accord with the norm of can. 305, and are subject to the governance of the same authority.

§2. It is also the responsibility of ecclesiastical authority, while observing the autonomy proper to private associations, to be watchful and take care that their energies are not dissipated and that their exercise of their apostolate is ordered toward the common good.

Can. 324 §1. A private association of the Christian faithful freely selects its own moderator and officials in accord with the norm of its statutes.

§2. A private association of the Christian faithful can freely choose a spiritual advisor, if it desires one, from among the priests legitimately exercising ministry in the diocese; however, he needs the confirmation of the local ordinary.

SELECTION SIX

From *The Lay Members of Christ: Faithful People*, John Paul II, (Boston: Daughters of St. Paul, 1988, pp. 70-73):

29. Church communion, already present and at work in the activities of the individual, finds its specific expression in the lay faithful's working together in groups, that is, in activities done with others in the course of their

responsible participation in the life and mission of the Church.

In recent days the phenomenon of lay people associating among themselves has taken on a character of particular variety and vitality. In some ways lay associations have always been present throughout the Church's history as various confraternities, third orders and sodalities testify even today. However, in modern times such lay groups have received a special stimulus, resulting in the birth and spread of a multiplicity of group forms: associations, groups, communities, movements. We can speak of *a new era of group endeavors* of the lay faithful. In fact, "alongside the traditional forming of associations, and at times coming from their very roots, movements and new sodalities have sprouted with a specific feature and purpose, so great is the richness and the versatility of resources that the Holy Spirit nourishes in the ecclesial community, and so great is the capacity of initiative and the generosity of our lay people" (John Paul II, August 23, 1987).

Oftentimes these lay groups show themselves to be *very diverse* from one another in various aspects, in their external structures, in their procedures and training methods and in the fields in which they work. However, they all come together with an all-inclusive and profound convergence when viewed from the perspective of their common purpose, that is, the responsible participation of all of them in the Church's mission of carrying forth the gospel of Christ—the source of hope for humanity and the renewal society.

The actual formation of groups of the lay faithful for spiritual purposes or for apostolic work comes from various sources and corresponds to different demands. In fact, their formation itself expresses the social nature of the person and for this reason leads to a more extensive and incisive effectiveness in work. In reality, a "cultural" effect can be accomplished through work done not so much by an individual alone but by an individual as a "social being," that is, as a member of a group, of a community, of an association or of a movement. Such work is, then, the source and stimulus leading to the transformation of the surroundings and society as well as the fruit and sign of every other transformation in this regard. This is particularly true in the context of a pluralistic and fragmented society—the case in so many parts of the world today—and in light of the problems which have become greatly complex and difficult. On the other hand, in a secularized world, above all, the various group forms of the apostolate can represent for many a precious help for the Christian life in remaining faithful to the demands of the gospel and to the commitment to the Church's mission and apostolate.

Beyond this, the profound reason that justifies and demands the lay faithful's forming of lay groups comes from a theology *based on ecclesiology*, as the Second Vatican Council clearly acknowledged in referring to the group apostolate as a "sign of communion and of unity of the Church of Christ" (AA 18).

It is a "sign" that must be manifested in relation to "communion" both in the internal and external aspects of the various group forms and in the wider context of the Christian community. As mentioned, this reason based on ecclesiology explains, on one hand, the "right" of lay associations to form, and on the other, the necessity of "criteria" for discerning the authenticity of the forms which such groups take in the Church.

First of all, the *freedom for lay people in the Church to form such groups* is to be acknowledged. Such liberty is a true and proper right that is not derived from any kind of "concession" by authority, but flows from the Sacrament of Baptism which calls the lay faithful to participate actively in the Church's communion and mission. In this regard the Council is quite clear: "As long as the proper relationship is kept to Church authority, the lay faithful have the right to found and run such associations and to join those already existing" (LG 37). A citation from the recently published Code of Canon Law affirms as well: "The Christian faithful are at liberty to found and govern associations for charitable and religious purposes or for the promotion of the Christian vocation in the world; they are free to hold meetings to pursue these purposes in common" (CIC, Can. 215).

It is a question of a freedom that is to be acknowledged and guaranteed by ecclesial authority and always and only to be exercised in Church communion. Consequently, the right of the lay faithful to form groups is essentially in relation to the Church's life of communion and to her mission.

SELECTION SEVEN

From "The Spiritual Mission of the Laity," by Jacques Maritain, *Communio*, 1965, pp. 194-196:

1. I do not intend to speak here of the *temporal* mission of laymen in civil society, or concerning the establishment by them of that "politique chretienne" to which I have alluded so frequently in the past. The capital importance of this temporal mission is evident. But these particular remarks are concerned with an entirely different matter: the *spiritual mission of the laity in the Church*. As a matter of fact, I much prefer the term "spiritual mission" to "apostolate." For the expression "apostolate of the laity," however exact it may be, has something ambiguous about it, and runs the risk of being understood *uniquely* as the participation of the laity in the mission proper to the hierarchy, or in the apostolate of the clergy.

I sometimes ask myself if during the last thirty years,

under the pressure of circumstances and practical needs, this question of the role of the laity in the life of the Mystical Body has not been developed in too empirical a manner and from too partial a point of view, without having been sufficiently thought through for itself and in all its fullness.

It may be true that I am somewhat misinformed. I have not read Father Congar's book on the theology of the laity. However I have listened to many discussions on the subject of the laity, and I come away from all these discussions with the impression that what we need is a study of the whole question, in all its ramifications, in which consideration is given not only to that form of witnessing and that spiritual mission (apostolic mission) which are peculiar to laymen, but also to those modalities peculiar to their interior life, to their spiritual trials, to their prayer (liturgical as well as private), and to their progress toward union with God and the perfection of charity, which is evidently what must come before all else, since progress toward perfection is prescribed for all: *estote perfecti...*

But let us get back to the subject. It seems to me (to return to what I suggested above) that any consideration of the role of the laity has taken as its point of departure something that is good and necessary, but which concerns only one single section of the laity; I mean Catholic Action and similar organizations, in such a way that, without ever realizing it clearly, we have never been able to escape from the perspective of a *participation in the apostolate proper to the clergy,* a perspective which has been broadened more and more, (as if it were ultimately capable of encompassing the laity in its entirety) all the while retaining from the same specific perspective, and continuing to see everything from the same original point of view. In the end there is a tendency to take for granted that, if the laity does have a spiritual mission and an apostolate, it could be nothing else but a participation in that mission and that apostolate proper to the clergy: all of which would end up in the formation, without its being specifically intended, of a "clerical" conception of the mission of the laity in the Church.

This is how I explain to myself the enormous, and almost exclusive, importance attached today (and I do not think it will be long before disillusionment sets in) to questions of organization, while at the same time many profound needs of the Christian soul remain unsatisfied.

It must not be forgotten, on the other hand, that the primordial role of the priest is not to organize laymen, but to bring them the Word of God. It must not be forgotten that it is never the group that creates a spirit.

2. Let it be clearly understood that Catholic Action and analogous groups organized by the clergy are *absolutely necessary* and fill an *urgent need* at the present time. I too insist on this necessity. But what I would insist on equally is that this involves only *one part, one segment*, of the Christian laity, and a certain particular mission which is the responsibility of this segment *considered specifically as auxiliary to the clergy*. The segment of the laity in question is directed to those activities which border on the domain of the ecclesiastical hierarchy, and arise, inasmuch as they share a condition common to all laymen, from the fact that these activities imply a *participation in the apostolate peculiar to the hierarchy*, and a *mandate received from the hierarchy*. It follows that it would be impossible, from this perspective, to conceive of the laity as a whole and of the spiritual mission that it has in the Church according to the condition common to all laymen.

In other words a distinction must be made, among laymen, between that work immanent to the Mystical Body carried on by certain laymen inasmuch as they have been given a *mission* or a *mandate* by the clergy,— and that work immanent to the Mystical Body carried on by those who *without having received from the clergy a mission or a mandate for some special activity* constitute basically the great multitude of the "faithful people of God."

Without doubt there exist in this immense multitude vast portions who are unfaithful to their calling, and more or less, sometimes completely, deChristianized. But there exists also living portions who are truly faithful, among whom the notion of a Christian laity is authentically realized, a great people animated by the faith and engaged in activities vital to the Mystical Body, people who are completely polarized by grace and charity.

The Christian laity as such,—independently of any participation, in certain given cadres, in the apostolate proper to the hierarchy,—has a witness to render and a spiritual mission in the Church. And those who share the common condition of the laity receive this mission, not from a special call or a special mandate from the hierarchy; they receive it from their baptism and their confirmation, in other words from the very fact that they are *members of Christ.*